A Pocketful of Whimsy

Wee Patchwork Gifts

by Kathleen Rindal Brooks

CHITRA PUBLICATIONS

Your Best Value in Quilting

Chitra Publications
2 Public Avenue
Montrose, Pennsylvania 18801-1220

First Printing: 1999

Library of Congress Cataloging-in-Publication Data

Brooks, Kathleen Rindal, Date
    A pocketful of whimsy : wee patchwork gifts / by Kathleen Rindal Brooks.
        p.   cm.
    ISBN 1-885588-27-5 (pbk.)
    1. Patchwork Patterns.   2. Gifts.   I. Title.
    TT835 .B7254 1999
    746.46'041--dc21

                                                                99-32787
                                                                CIP

Edited by: Debra Feece
Design and Illustrations: Diane M. Albeck-Grick
Cover Photography: Guy Cali Associates, Inc., Clarks Summit, Pennsylvania
Inside Photography: Guy Cali Associates, Inc., Clarks Summit, Pennsylvania

Our Mission Statement:

*We publish quality quilting magazines and books
that recognize, promote and inspire self-expression.
We are dedicated to serving our customers
with respect, kindness and efficiency.*

Dedication: for Travis, Jordan and Hayley, my best gifts

Introduction

I didn't sit down to write this book. It "appeared," one gift at a time. If you're like me, you have a long list of friends who would treasure a quilted gift. Since there aren't enough hours in the day to make quilts for all of them, this book will show you ways to put a little patchwork into each friend's hands.

A few of my patterns were inspired by antique originals—some of which I am lucky enough to own. A few ideas I mooched from friends. The rest I designed with someone special in mind.

Most of these projects can be stitched in an afternoon.

Sew a tiny piece of patchwork, carrying thoughts of friendship—something to slip into a handbag or tuck into a pocket—their own pocketful of whimsy.

Kathleen

"Every good and perfect gift is from above."
James 1:16

Table of Contents

General Techniques

Fabric

If choosing fabrics tends to make you hyperventilate, relax! Generally, a scrap of this and a piece of that is just about all you'll need for these projects. (Of course, on the downside, this means you'll have one less excuse for buying more fabric.)

Look at this as an opportunity to use old fabrics in a new way or a chance to use unusual fabrics that, although appealing, never seem to fit comfortably into your quilts. This is also a way to showcase a "lucky find" or that last remaining scrap of a treasured fabric.

Since these projects require a limited number of fabrics, this is a good time to play. Experiment with colors outside of your usual palette. Be a little unpredictable. Choose fabrics in colors and styles that may not be your favorite, but fit the special person who will receive your gift.

Piecing with a variety of prints can create a wonderful texture on the surface of your project. A mixture of different patterns—botanicals, geometrics, checks, stripes and plaids—provides energy and dimension. Although you may be tempted to reach for those tried and true small scale prints, varying the scale of your prints will give your work zing.

Conversational prints (fabrics printed with small objects or images) and other specialty fabrics are another way to add fun and focus to a project. Pull out all those ribbon-tied fat quarter bundles that you couldn't resist but haven't touched—and put them to work!

To visualize how a particular fabric might look once it is pieced into your project, prepare paper windows the size and shape of your patches, then lay a window over your fabric to help you see how that motif or pattern will look. (See "Look in the Window" on the opposite page.)

Printing Fabric!

You might want to personalize some of the projects with a word, phrase, friend's name or initials. If you don't have fabric with the appropriate letters, you can print your own.

Use your computer and a laser or inkjet printer to print fabric.

Here's how:
- Press a piece of freezer paper to a piece of muslin, then trim both paper and fabric to the size of the printer paper.
- Feed it through the printer, muslin side up (for most printers).
- To set the ink, place a piece of aluminum foil over the image and press on top of the foil.

Tools

The proper tools make any job simpler. There are endless gadgets on the market, but here are a few of my favorites.

- ✗ Rotary cutter
- ✗ Specialty rulers—bias square, large square, rectangular ruler
- ✗ Clover flower head pins
- ✗ Graph paper: quarter-inch grid, matched
- ✗ Vellum or Easy Piece for Foundations
- ✗ Graphite paper
- ✗ Washout marker
- ✗ Loop turner

Techniques

When working with small pieces, traditional piecing methods leave too much room for error. There are a couple of ways to solve this problem. Depending on which project I'm making, I generally resort to either downsizing or to foundation piecing. Each method maximizes accuracy in its own way.

Downsizing

When two small patches need to be joined, such as in the Pinwheels and Four Patches for the Chatelaine, I cut my fabric as if for a larger block and sew the pieces together with a 1/4" seam. Press the seams to one side, then trim the seams to 1/8" and rotary cut the block to size. For example, if the project requires a 1" Four Patch block, I make a 3" Four Patch block and then cut it down to the required 1" size.

Foundation Piecing

My favorite construction method is foundation piecing. Many of the projects in this book utilize this simple and accurate technique.

When using this technique, begin by photocopying or tracing the foundation pattern onto lightweight paper. I have always used vellum, a translucent drafting paper (available at art or drafting supply stores). However, there are a couple of new foundation papers on the market (Easy Piece, for example) which I also like and which are made specifically for paper piecing. As with vellum, they can also be used in photocopiers or laser printers, and the pattern can be seen on both sides. I do not recommend copying onto tracing paper because it is not durable enough to withstand the ripping out of stitches, if that's necessary. An additional benefit, and the primary reason to use vellum or Easy Piece, is that it is durable enough to withstand "un-sewing" but still tears away easily and cleanly when piecing is complete.

If you don't have access to vellum or one of the other specialty papers designed for this purpose, you can use graphite paper to transfer the design to the reverse side of your regular photocopy or traced pattern. (Graphite paper, although similar to carbon paper, does not rub off on fingers or fabric.) Place the graphite paper, graphite side against the back of the pattern, and trace over the pattern using a mechanical pencil with the lead removed. This will transfer the pattern to the back without pencil marks blurring the sewing lines on the front. It's okay if your tracing is a bit imprecise since your sewing will follow the photocopied pattern; the traced lines simply help you place your fabrics accurately.

Once the paper pattern is ready, you can begin sewing. In preparation, thread your sewing machine with a neutral (gray or beige) color thread. Set the stitch length at 15-20 stitches per inch (or at 2.0 on a European machine); a small stitch length perforates the paper enough to enable you to tear it away more easily later. Do not be tempted to set the stitch length too short or you risk the paper detaching too early.

To begin the actual piecing, locate the first piece (#1) on your paper pattern, then rough cut a scrap of fabric at least 1/4" larger on all sides than the size of area #1. Lay the fabric patch right side up, covering section #1. Rough cut a second scrap of fabric large enough to cover area #2 and extend beyond it at least 1/4" on all sides. Place this piece right side up, covering pattern area #2. Check its placement before flipping piece #2 right side down on top of piece #1. Secure both pieces together with a pin. (Using Clover flower head pins allows the work to lie flat in the next step.) Turn the entire unit over and sew along the pattern line between #1 and #2, beginning and ending just a few stitches beyond each end of the line. Clip the threads and trim the seam allowance to 1/8", taking care not to cut the foundation. Press the fabrics open. Continue adding pieces in numerical sequence, remembering to trim the seam allowances and press as you go, until your block is complete. Baste around the edges of the block within the 1/4" seam allowance to hold fabrics in place, if desired. Now correct your block size by trimming it to the size of the finished block plus a 1/4" seam allowance on each side.

Once all your blocks are complete, you can assemble the project. If you need to, give your blocks a final pressing now. *Never ever re-press your patchwork once the paper has been removed or you risk hopelessly distorting all your perfect piecing!*

After stitching the blocks to each other, it's time to remove the paper. At this stage, it is helpful to remember all the time and frustration that paper piecing has saved you. With your favorite snacks within reach, park yourself in a comfy chair and flip on "the tube." Carefully tear away the paper pieces one by one. Stubborn fragments can be coaxed free after a light misting of water from a spray bottle. (Remember, no re-pressing.)

Batting

For many of these projects, any low loft batting will do. But for some of these pieces, I specifically recommend using Hobbs Thermore batting. Thermore provides body to the finished piece while still maintaining its flatness. I do not recommend using flannel in place of batting. Insufficient loft results in a finished look that is too flat, causing your quilting stitch to look more like an embroidered running stitch.

Look in the Window

Use paper or cardboard "windows" to get an idea of how a novelty print will work to its best advantage in your project.

Here's how:
- Make the outside dimensions of the window frame the size and shape of the pattern piece, including seam allowances.
- Make the inside dimensions the size and shape of the finished quilt piece.
- Place the window on the right side of your fabric and adjust as desired.
- When the fabric in the window appears as you would like it in the finished project, simply trace around the outside edge and cut.

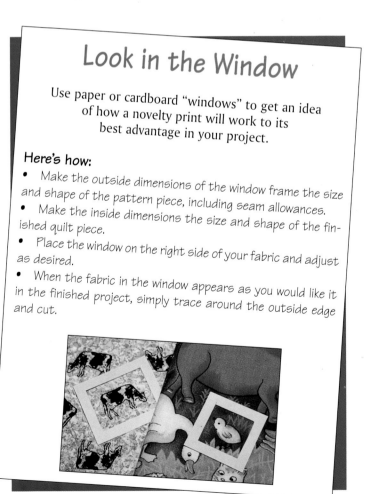

Chatelaine

Add a collection of antique sewing implements and it serves as a piece of "jewelry."

Make a patchwork chatelaine to keep your quilting tools close at hand. For quilters "on the road," this is a functional piece designed to allow easy access to your scissors, seam ripper, and a spool of thread.

SIZE: 1" x 41"

MATERIALS
- Assorted light, medium and dark print and plaid scraps

TIP: *To highlight the tiny patchwork, use intense colors and choose high contrast for adjacent pieces.*
- 1/2" button
- 1 1/2" length of "baby" elastic (1/8" wide)
- Needlework tools (examples: small pincushion, needlecase, thimble holder, thread clippers, small scissors, thread)
- Foundation paper
- Optional thimble and scissors charms

TIP: *Custom fit your chatelaine by laying a tape measure around your neck and over your shoulders to determine a comfortable length. Keep in mind that the tools which hang off the ends will need additional clearance (so they won't be laying in your lap!) To lengthen the chatelaine, piece additional sections and add them to the midpoint. To shorten, leave out a section or two.*

CUTTING
Pattern pieces are full size and include a 1/4" seam allowance, as do all dimension given.
- Cut 14: 2 1/4" squares, dark prints, then cut them in half diagonally to yield 28 triangles, for the Pinwheel blocks
- Cut 14: 2 1/4" squares, light prints, then cut them in half diagonally to yield 28 triangles, for the Pinwheel blocks
- Cut 12: 1 1/2" squares, assorted dark prints, for the Four Patch blocks
- Cut 1: 1 1/4" x 1 1/2" rectangle, dark plaid or check
- Cut 1: end piece K, plaid
- Cut 1: end piece L, plaid
- Cut 5: 1" x 9" bias strips, plaids

DIRECTIONS
This chatelaine combines a number of simple piecing techniques. Follow the Foundation Piecing instructions in General Techniques *to make the foundations and to piece the blocks. Make one foundation each from patterns A, B, D, E, G, H, I, and J. Make 2 from pattern C. Make 4 from pattern F. The foundation patterns are on page 8.*

For foundations A, B, C:
- Use assorted dark prints for the shaded areas of each foundation. Use assorted light prints for the remaining areas.

For foundation D:
- Use the following fabrics in these positions:
    1 through 5 - assorted medium and dark prints
    6 - plaid

For foundations E, G and J:
- Use assorted medium and dark prints in all positions.

For each of 2 foundation F's:

TIP: *The #1 position is a good place to highlight tiny motifs.*
- Use the following fabrics in these positions:
    1 - light print
    2 through 5 - one dark print

For the remaining foundation F's:
- Use the following fabrics in these positions:
    1 - dark print
    2 through 5 - one light print

For foundation H:
- Use the following fabrics in these positions:
    1 - blue print
    2 - red print
    3, 4, 5 - light print

For foundation I:
- Use the following fabrics in these positions:
    1 - light print
    2, 3, 4 - blue print
    5 through 10 - assorted medium and dark prints
    11 - plaid

For the Pinwheel blocks and Four Patch blocks:
Follow the Downsizing instructions in General Techniques *to construct the Pinwheel blocks and Four Patch blocks.*
- Make 7 Pinwheel blocks, using assorted dark and light triangles. Trim each block to 1 1/2" square.

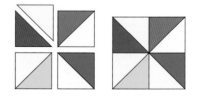

- Make 3 Four Patch blocks, using the 1 1/2" assorted dark print squares. Trim each block to 1 1/2" square.

ASSEMBLY

- Following the diagrams, stitch the foundations, Pinwheel blocks and Four Patch blocks together to make sections, as shown. Stitch the 1 1/4" x 1 1/2" dark plaid or check rectangle to the end of Section 1.

- Fold the 1 1/2" length of baby elastic in half. Baste the elastic loop (facing in, with the ends toward the raw edge of the patchwork) to the curved end of piece K. The elastic loop should extend 1/2" beyond the seamline.
- With right sides together, center the chatelaine front on the backing. Stitch them together around the outside of the chatelaine front, using a 1/4" seam allowance.
- Trim the backing to match the edges of the chatelaine front.
- Remove the paper foundations now.
- Carefully turn the chatelaine right side out through the opening in the backing.

TIP: *While it is possible to leave an opening at the side to turn your work, it is difficult to get a smooth finish when hand stitching the opening closed.*

- Press. Hand stitch the opening closed.

- Fold a 1" x 9" plaid bias strip in half lengthwise, right side in. Stitch 1/4" from the long raw edge to make a tube. Trim the seam allowance to 1/8" and turn the tube right side out **NOTE:** *Use a loop turner for ease in turning.* Tuck in the ends and hand stitch them closed. Make 5.
- Stitch the center of one tie to the short plaid end of the chatelaine. Tie a silver pin cushion or a strawberry to this end. (It's best to keep your pins in this pincushion and your needles in the needlecase—we don't want the needles poking you!)
- Sew the 1/2" button to the place indicated on the pattern. Fold the bottom up and slip the elastic loop over the button.
- Use the remaining bias ties to slip through the handle of your scissors, the hole in your spool of thread, etc. Tie the tools you need to this end of the chatelaine.
- Attach a needlecase, thimble holder and charms to the unpieced sections.

TIP: *I use an antique stamp holder to store my tiny quilting needles. To prevent them from slipping out the gap, I placed a flat magnet with the sticky back inside the stamp holder.*

- Join the sections, matching symbols (see the Assembly Diagram), to make one long continuous piece of patchwork for the chatelaine front.
- Stitch the plaid K to the end of Section 1 and the plaid L to the end of Section 5.

FINISHING

- For the backing, cut random lengths of 2"-wide prints and plaids. Join them to equal the length of the chatelaine front. Leave a 1" opening between two sections of the backing near the center, backstitching each seam to secure.

Assembly Diagram

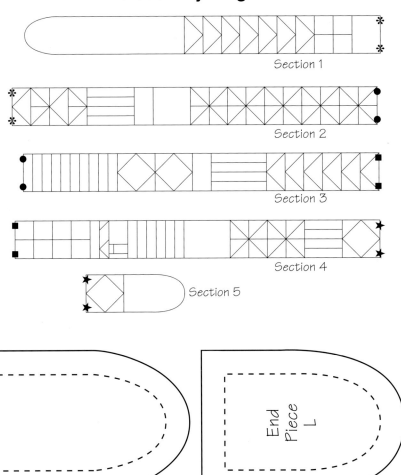

Full-Size Patterns for Chatelaine

(The patterns are continued on page 8.)

End Piece K

End Piece L

Full-Size Foundation Patterns for Chatelaine

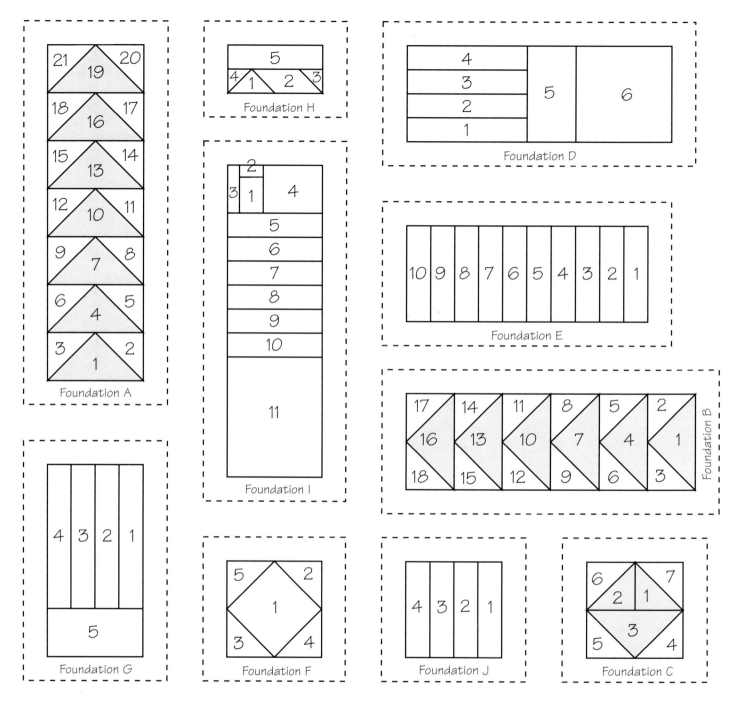

Full-Size Foundation Pattern for Bookmark

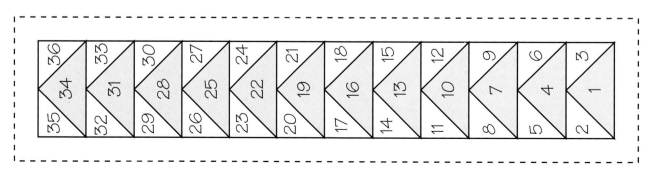

Bookmark

Give these flying geese to
a special teacher, friend or relative.
They'll think of you every time
they turn a page.

This simple paper-pieced design is so quick and versatile that after you stitch the first one, you won't want to stop.

SIZE: 1 3/4" x 6 3/4"

MATERIALS
- 12 dark print scraps for the "geese"
TIP: *Use tiny conversation prints to add personality to your bookmark. Use fabric printed with letters to spell out the recipient's name. (See "Look in the Window" in General Techniques on page 5.)*
- 12 light print scraps for the background
- Scrap of dark print at least 3" x 7" for the border
- 2 print scraps at least 2 1/2" x 4" for the backing
- Paper for the foundation
- Optional: decorative bead and 4" length of 1/8"-wide ribbon

CUTTING
Dimensions include a 1/4" seam allowance.
- Cut 12: 1" x 1 1/2" rectangles, dark scraps, for the "geese"
- Cut 12: 1 1/2" squares, assorted light prints, for the background, then cut them in half diagonally to yield 24 triangles
- Cut 2: 7/8" x 6 1/2" strips, dark print, for the border
- Cut 2: 7/8" x 2 1/2" strips, dark print, for the border
- Cut 2: 2 1/2" x 4" rectangles, prints, for the backing

DIRECTIONS
Follow the Foundation Piecing instructions in General Techniques to make the foundation and to piece the block. Make one foundation from the pattern on page 8.
- Use the 1" x 1 1/2" dark print rectangles for the shaded areas of the foundation. Use the light print triangles for the remaining areas.
- Stitch the 7/8" x 6 1/2" dark print strips to the sides of the patchwork.
- Stitch the 7/8" x 2 1/2" dark print strips to the top and bottom of the patchwork.
- Place the 2 1/2" x 4" print rectangles right sides together and stitch, leaving a 1" opening in the center of the seam, as shown. Backstitch at each end of both seams to secure.

- Open the backing and press the seam allowance to one side.

- Center the patchwork on the backing, right sides together. Stitch all the way around the outside with a 1/4" seam allowance.

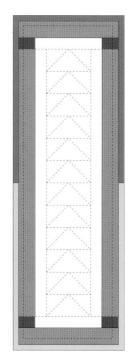

- Remove the paper foundation now.
- Trim seam allowances to a scant 1/4". Trim the corners diagonally.
- Turn the bookmark right side out through the opening in the backing.
- Hand stitch the opening closed.

Bookcover

Simple piecing makes it easy to size
this cover to fit any book.

An address book, diary, blank book or your latest paperback novel—you won't mind leaving it lying around when it looks this good. (Well, maybe not your diary...)

SIZE: Custom sized to fit your book.

MATERIALS
• Address book, photo album, paperback or blank book
• 50-100 fabric scraps
• 1/4 yard lining (1/2 yard if your book is more than 8" in height)
• 3-5 vertical prints for sashing (border prints in different widths work well)
• Thin batting

PLANNING
• Begin by taking some simple measurements and formulating a general plan for the finished cover.
• Measure your book from the edge of the front cover, around the spine, to the edge of the back cover. The final width of your patchwork will be this measurement plus at least 4" for overlap inside the book covers (2" at each end). The larger the book, the greater the overlap will need to be in order to keep the cover in place.

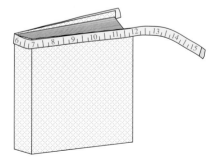

• Measure the cover of your book from top to bottom and add 1 1/2" (1" for ease and 1/2" for the seam allowances). This measurement will be the final height of your patchwork. Write down the height

and width measurements.
• The bookcover will be made from vertical sashing strips and vertical stacks of horizontally stitched rectangles. Now that you have determined the height and width of your patchwork, choose the vertical sashing strips that will be sewn between the vertical stacks of piecing. For the average address book, 5 sashing strips work well. For a small book, 3 strips may be sufficient.

PIECING
• Cut the vertical sashing strips any width you choose, remembering to add a 1/4" seam allowance to each side. The length of these strips should be the same as your vertical patchwork measurement. Lay these strips side by side and measure their total width, minus the seam allowances. (This will give you their finished measurement.)
• Subtract that number from the total width of your patchwork. The combined finished width of your vertical patchwork stacks will need to equal this measurement.
• Begin sewing random width strips of fabric, one on top of another, until the length of the patchwork stack equals the patchwork height measurement. Use a rotary cutter to even the edges of the stack.

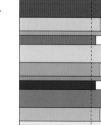

• Stitch a vertical sashing strip to one side of the patchwork stack. Construct another patchwork stack the same length as the first strip of vertical sash-

ing. Stitch this patchwork stack to the other side of the vertical sashing. Continue in this manner, trimming the width of the patchwork stacks as desired to create balanced sections.

TIP: *The first and last sections need to include the 2" (or larger) overlap that will go inside the book covers. I used vertical sashing strips for these sections. The center section that covers the spine of the book should be wide enough to wrap around the spine and extend onto the front and back of the book.*

• Once your patchwork is complete, recheck its measurements. Remember, it should measure the width of your book plus at least 4" and the height plus 1 1/2".
• Rough cut a piece of fabric for the lining at least 1/4" larger on all sides than the patchwork. Cut a piece of thin batting the same size as the lining.
• Layer the: batting; lining, right side up on the batting; and the patchwork, right side down on the lining. Pin the layers. Leaving an opening on one short side, sew around the edges using a 1/4" seam allowance measured from the edge of the patchwork. Trim the batting close to the stitching line. Trim the lining even with the edges of the patchwork.

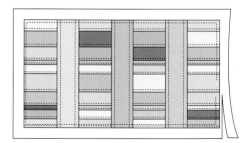

• Turn the book cover right side out.

Press. Handstitch the opening closed.
- Lay the patchwork cover on your work surface, lining side up. Center the opened book on the patchwork cover and fold the patchwork ends inside the book covers. Adjust the patchwork, keeping the book centered and making sure the ends of the book cover extend to the folds when the book is closed.
- Carefully remove the book and pin the end flaps in place. Topstitch 1/8" from

the edges by hand or machine, as shown, securing the end flaps.

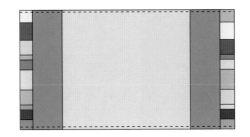

- To insert the book after the cover is complete, fold the book back gently (against the spine—the way teachers tell you never to do) and slip the covers into the end flaps.

Eyeglass Case

Don't miss the details.

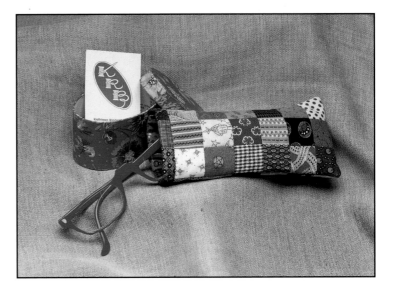

Give them something to really look at. Keep your specs safe and handy inside this arty case. Fun fabrics make the case.

SIZE: 3" x 6 1/2"

MATERIALS
Yardage is estimated for 44" fabric.
- Assorted print scraps
- 4" x 14" piece of flannel for the lining
- 4" x 14" piece of thin batting

CUTTING
Dimensions include a 1/4" seam allowance.
- Cut 42: 1 1/2" squares, assorted print scraps
- Cut 2: 3 1/2" x 6 1/2" rectangles, flannel
- Cut 2: 3 1/2" x 7 1/2" rectangles, thin batting

DIRECTIONS
For the front:
- Stitch three 1 1/2" squares together to make Row 1. Press the seam allowances in one direction. Make 4.
- Stitch 3 squares together to make Row 2. Press the seam allowances in the opposite direction. Make 3.
- Join the rows, alternating Rows 1 and

2 so the seams butt against each other. Press the seam allowances between the rows toward the bottom.
For the back:
- Piece the back of the eyeglass case in the same manner, pressing the seam allowances between the rows toward the top.

ASSEMBLY
- Lay the front piece right side up on a 3 1/2" x 7 1/2" rectangle of batting, aligning the edges. Lay a flannel rectangle on top of the patchwork, right side down, with the top and side edges even. (The lining will be shorter, so the patchwork will be sticking out at the bottom.) Sew across the top edge with a 1/4" seam allowance. Repeat for the back piece. Open the units and press the seams toward the patchwork (including the batting seam allowances.)

- Lay the front unit and the back unit right sides together. The patchwork should be facing patchwork and the lining should be facing lining. Stitch around the outside edges through all layers with a 1/4" seam allowance, leaving a 1 1/2" opening in the side of the lining.
- Turn right side out through the opening in the side of the lining. Press. Hand stitch the opening closed. Tuck the lining inside the eyeglass case. Half of the top row of patchwork will fold inside the case and become part of the lining. Topstitch around the top edge of the case by machine or quilt around the top edge by hand.

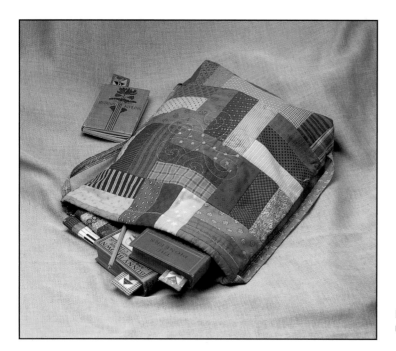

Backpack

Hide those on-the-go odds and ends
in this playful pack.

Pull it all together and take it along. This handy tote makes a fashion statement that's sure to delight any traveler.

SIZE: 14" x 18"

MATERIALS

Yardage is estimated for 44" fabric.
• Assorted print fabrics totaling approximately 1 yard
• 1 yard print for the lining and straps
• 23" x 35" piece of thin batting (optional)

CUTTING

Dimensions include a 1/4" seam allowance.
• Cut 36: 2 1/4" x 12" strips, assorted prints
• Cut 2: 17" x 22" rectangles, print, for the lining
• Cut 2: 2 1/2" x 32" strips, print, for the straps
• Cut 2: 17" x 22" rectangles of batting

DIRECTIONS

• Stitch three 2 1/4" x 12" assorted print strips together along their length. Press the seam allowances in one direction. Cut two 5 3/4" blocks from the pieced unit. One block will be used in the front of the backpack and one block will be used in the back.
• In the same manner, make 11 more 3-strip units and cut 2 blocks from each. Separate them as before into 2 groups, one for the front and one for the back.

• Lay out the 12 blocks for the front in 4 rows of 3 alternating the blocks, as shown.

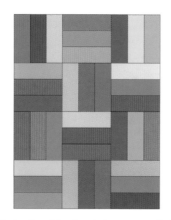

• Stitch the blocks into rows. Join the rows.
• Arrange the remaining 12 blocks for the back and join them in the same manner.

ASSEMBLY

• Layer a lining rectangle right side down, a piece of batting on top (if desired), and the patchwork front right side up. Smooth the layers and pin. If desired, machine quilt in the ditch along the seamlines. Trim the batting and lining even with the edges of the patchwork. Serge or zigzag all 4 edges of the patchwork sandwich. Repeat for the back.
TIP: *When finishing the edges, stitch with the lining up, patchwork down. This will help ease the patchwork seams and prevent "lumps" where the seams come together.*
• Fold a 2 1/2" x 32" print strip in half lengthwise, right side in. Stitch the long side and turn it right side out. Make 2.
NOTE: *Use a loop turner for ease in turning.*
TIP: *For more stable straps, you may want to*

add a layer of batting to this step. Cut batting 1 1/8" wide x 32" long. Lay a batting strip on the folded strip and catch it in the seam as you sew.
• Topstitch 1/8" from the long edges of each strap. Topstitch again 1/4" from the long edges. Make sure the straps are the same length. If one is longer than the other, trim it to match.
• Lay the front of the bag right side up. Lay the straps at the sides. 3 1/2" from the bottom, with the raw edges even. Baste the straps to the front.

• Place the front and back of the bag right sides together. Be sure to place the back of the bag so the blocks alternate direction with the adjoining blocks at the sides. Leaving a 1" opening 1 1/2" from the top edge on each side, stitch the side and bottom seams. (Be careful not to catch the loose ends of the straps in the seams.)

- Press the side seams open. Topstitch 1/8" around the opening in the side seams.

- To give dimension to the bag, stitch across each bottom corner. Do this by flattening out the bottom of the bag so the bottom seam and side seams are in alignment. (A corner triangle is formed at each end.) Stitch across one corner, perpendicular to the bottom seam. This seam should be about 2" from the point and be about 3 1/2" long. Stitch the other bottom corner in the same manner.
- Turn the bag right side out.
- Press under 1/4" along the top edge of the backpack. Press the folded edge 1 1/4" to the inside of the bag. Pin. Stitch 1/8" from the folded edge, forming a casing.

TIP: *I used a medium zigzag stitch to stitch the casing to help ease the bulkiness of the batting.*
- Thread the loose end of the strap through the casing opening on the same side seam and come out the opposite casing opening.

TIP: *Thread the strap through the casing with a diaper pin or large safety pin. OR Push a loop turner through the casing, beginning at the opposite end and coming out where you want to begin threading. Attach the loop turner to the end of the strap and pull it through the casing. Check to be sure the strap is not twisted within the casing.*

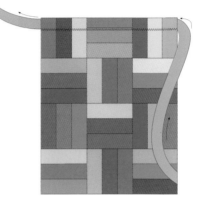

- Fold the raw edge of the strap under and tuck it flat into the casing opening (gently pull the strap back through but don't let the end disappear completely into the casing). Pin it in place and stitch the folded end to the backpack inside the casing. This seems a little tricky at first, but you can spread the opening and just stitch inside it to secure the strap.

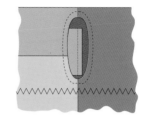

- Thread the remaining strap through the other side of the casing. Again, begin at the opening at the same side seam the strap is attached to and come out the opposite side. Fold under and secure the end of the strap inside the opening as you did for the other side.
- To close your backpack, pull on the straps and the top will gather closed.

"Huswif"

Make history yourself. Hang your huswif on the wall or carry it with you "into the field."

Many a Civil War soldier went off to battle with a "huswif" tucked into the pocket of his uniform. The useful item was filled with sewing supplies and an extra button or two for doing his own mending while away from home.

SIZE: 5" x 18"

MATERIALS
TIP: *A civil war era antique inspired this pattern. For an authentic look, take advantage of the wonderful reproduction fabrics on the market.*
- Print fabric at least 6" x 18" for the base foundation **NOTE:** *The pockets will be sewn to this piece which is also the back.*
- 9 print scraps, each at least 6" x 5", for the pockets

- 3/4" diameter plastic ring
- Fat quarter (18" x 22") stripe, for the binding

CUTTING
The pattern piece includes a 1/4" seam allowance, as do all dimensions given.
- Cut 1: 6" x 18" rectangle, print, for the base foundation
- Cut 1: A, for the top
- Cut 7: 4 1/2" x 6" rectangles, for the pockets

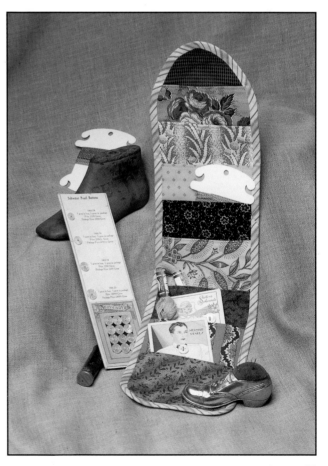

- Cut 1: 3 1/4" x 6" rectangle, for the bottom pocket
- Cut 2: 1 1/4" x 24" bias strips, stripe, for the binding

DIRECTIONS

- Narrow hem one long edge of each of the 8 pockets in the following manner: press the edge under 1/4". Fold the raw edge under to meet the pressed line and stitch along the fold.

- Lay the base foundation right side down. Beginning at the top, center piece A right side down on the base foundation, 4 inches from the top, as shown. Stitch across, using a 1/4" seam allowance. Fold piece A up and press.
- Lay a pocket rectangle 2" below the first stitching line, right side down, with the raw edge toward the top. Stitch across, as before. Fold the pocket up and press.

- Continue adding 6 more pockets in the same way, each approximately 2" lower than the previous pocket. **TIP:** *For a folksy style, vary the placement slightly so each pocket will appear to differ in size.*

- Lay the bottom pocket rectangle on the base foundation, right side up and aligning the raw edges, as shown. Baste across the bottom, 1/8" from the edge. Trim each bottom corner to create a slight curve.
- Trim the top edge of the base foundation even with the curve of piece A. Trim the unit to 5" wide. Beginning at the bottom, baste along the sides 1/8" from the edges to hold the pockets in place.
- Join the 2 bias binding strips end to end. Starting 1" from the end, stitch the binding to the "Huswif" with a 1/4" seam allowance. Stop stitching 1" from the starting point.
- Fold the ends of the bias strip toward the wrong side at the point where they meet. Pinch the folds to make creases. Trim the excess from each end, leaving a 1/4" seam allowance.

- Place the ends of the binding strip right sides together and stitch on the crease.
- Finish stitching the binding to the "Huswif".

- Turn the binding toward the back of the "Huswif." Fold the raw edge of the binding under 1/4" and hand stitch it in place along the stitching line.
- Stitch the plastic ring to the back, near the top, to hang your "Huswif."

Full-Size Pattern for "Huswif"

A

Napkin Rings

Dress your table for every occasion.

Add a touch of whimsy to your table with simple napkin rings secured with tiny buttons.

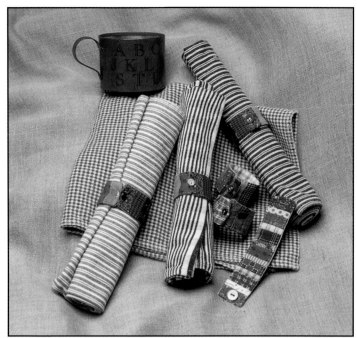

SIZE: 1 1/4" x 5"

MATERIALS
- Assorted fabric scraps
- Paper for foundations
- 1/4" button
- Thin batting

CUTTING

Dimensions include a 1/4" seam allowance.
- Cut 1: 1 3/4" x 5 1/2" strip, print, for the backing
- Cut 1: 2 1/4" x 6" strip, thin batting

PIECING

Follow the Foundation Piecing instructions in General Techniques *to make and piece the foundation. Make one foundation from either of the napkin ring patterns.*
- Lay the paper foundation marked side down. Center the 2 1/4" x 6" rectangle of batting on top of the paper. Stitching through both the paper and the batting, piece as you would any foundation pattern. Use assorted print scraps in all positions.
- Trim all layers on the broken line.
- Lay the 1 3/4" x 5 1/2" backing rectangle on the sewn unit, right sides together. Stitch the long sides and one short side, leaving one end open. Trim the seam allowance to a scant 1/4".
- Remove the paper foundation. Turn the napkin ring right side out and press. Tuck the seam allowance in and hand stitch the opening closed.
- Hand stitch along each long side with a running stitch.
- Stitch a buttonhole near one short end and sew a button on the opposite end.

Other ideas:
Don't do buttonholes?
- Use a small piece of Velcro to close the napkin ring instead.
- Shape the unit into a ring, overlapping the ends slightly and hand stitch the ring closed.
- Overlap the ends and sew on a button through both layers.

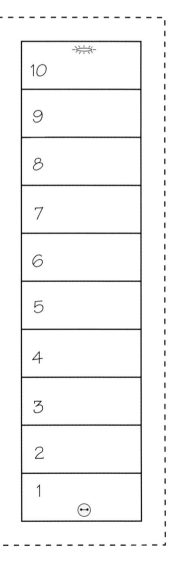

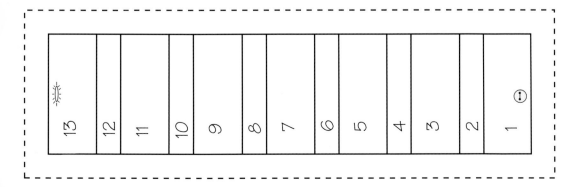

Full-Size Foundation Patterns for Napking Rings

Tote Bag

This tiny tote will carry
your latest needlework
project (or your lunch) in style.

This original gift came into my hands from my creative friend, Kathy Gillespie.

SIZE: 7 1/2" x 6 1/2" x 4"

MATERIALS

Yardage is estimated for 44" fabric.
- 80 print scraps, each at least 3" square
- 1/4 yard print fabric for the lining
- 1/8 yard each of 2 print fabrics for the side panels

TIP: *Just for fun, you may want to cut the panels from different fabrics.*
- 3" x 15" piece of print fabric for the handles
- 8" x 22" piece of thin batting
- 3 1/2" x 6" piece of cardboard
- Paper for foundations

CUTTING

Pattern pieces include a 1/4" seam allowance as do all dimensions given.
- Cut 2: 1 1/2" x 15" strips, print, for the handles
- Cut 4: B, prints, for the side panels (two for the outside, two for the lining)
- Cut 1: 8" x 22" rectangle, print, for the lining
- Cut 1: 8" x 22" rectangle, thin batting
- Cut 2: 4" x 6 1/2" rectangles, print

DIRECTIONS

Follow the foundation piecing instructions in General Techniques *to make the foundations and to piece the blocks. Make 5 foundations from the triangle row pattern for the even numbered rows. Turn the pattern over and make 5 more foundations from it for the odd numbered rows.* **NOTE:** *If you prefer to traditionally piece the rows, refer to "For Traditionally Pieced Rows" on page 18.*

For each of 5 odd numbered rows:
- Using assorted prints in all positions, piece each row from right to left.

For each of 5 even numbered rows:
- Using assorted prints in all positions, piece each row from left to right.
- Stitch the foundation pieced rows together, alternating even and odd numbered rows.

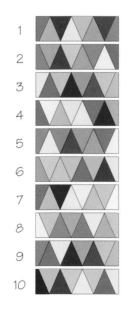

For the handles and lining:
- Fold a 1 1/2" x 15" print strip in half lengthwise, right side in. Stitch the long side, using a 1/4" seam allowance. Turn the handle right side out. **NOTE:** *Use a loop turner for ease in turning.*
- Topstitch the long sides 1/16" from the edges. Make 2.
- Place a print panel B and a print lining B right sides together. Stitch, leaving an opening for turning. Turn right side out. Press. Hand stitch the opening closed. Repeat with the remaining side panel B and lining B.

ASSEMBLY

- Baste the handles to the top and bottom of the pieced unit with the raw edges together, about 1/2" away from the side seams. Be careful not to twist the handles.

- Layer the 8" x 22" lining rectangle, right side up on top of the 8" x 22" piece of batting. Center the patchwork right side down on top of the lining. Stitch around the outside, leaving an opening on one side for turning.
- Trim the batting close to the stitching. Trim the lining, leaving a 1/4" seam allowance. Turn right side out through the opening and press. Hand stitch the opening closed.
- Now for the tricky part! Bend the patchwork rectangle to form the shape of the bag and pin or baste a side panel in place along the edge, wrong sides together. Use care when you are fitting these pieces together so the top edges of the bag and the side panel will be even.

Topstitch the side panel and the bag together, 1/4" from the edge.

- Repeat for the other side panel.
- Place the 4" x 6 1/2" rectangles of lining fabric, right sides together. Stitch both long sides and one short side to make a pocket.

- Turn the pocket right side out. Slip the 3 1/2" x 6" piece of cardboard inside. Fold the raw edges to the inside. Topstitch or hand stitch the opening closed. Place the covered cardboard in the bottom of the bag.

Full-Size Patterns for Totebag

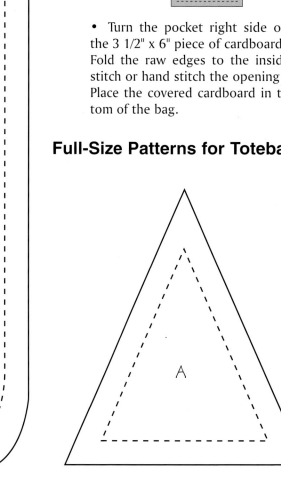

Triangle Row Foundation Pattern

Top

B

1 2 3 4 5 6 7 8

A

For Traditionally Pieced Rows:
CUTTING
Pattern piece A on page 17 is full size and includes a 1/4" seam allowance, as do all dimensions given.
• Cut 80: A, assorted prints
NOTE: *Cut these A's only if you prefer to traditionally piece the rows of triangles.*

To piece the triangle rows:
• Stitch 8 triangle A's into a row, alternating them, as shown. Make 10 rows.

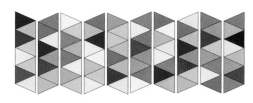

• Join the rows.
• Trim the long sides with a rotary cutter so the width measures 7", keeping the patchwork centered.

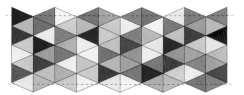

• Return to the Directions on page 16, beginning with "For the handles and lining".

Drawstring Pouch

Even if you don't own a marble collection, you'll want one of these!

Use this tiny pouch to hold everything from sea shells to needlework tools—or as gift wrapping for a special treasure. Mine holds my antique bakelite button collection.

SIZE: 3" x 5"

MATERIALS
• Assorted medium and dark print scraps
• Print for the lining, at least 6" x 8 1/2"
• 6" square of print fabric for the casing
• Print fabric for the ties, at least 1 3/4" x 13" (or use two 13" lengths of ribbon)
• 3" square of fusible interfacing
• Paper for foundations

CUTTING
Pattern pieces are full size and include a 1/4" seam allowance, as do all dimensions given.
• Cut 2: 1 3/4" x 4 1/2" bias strips, print, for the casing
• Cut 2: 7/8" x 13" strips, print, for the ties
• Cut 1: 6" x 8 1/2" rectangle, print, for the lining
• Cut 2: A, assorted prints, (one for the lining, one for the pouch)
• Cut 1: B, fusible interfacing.

DIRECTIONS
Follow the foundation piecing instructions in General Techniques *to make the foundations and to piece the blocks. Make 6 foundations from the Cracker pattern on the opposite page.*
To piece the blocks:
• Use assorted print scraps in all positions.
• After piecing the foundations, stitch 3 blocks together to form a row. Make 2 rows. Join the rows.

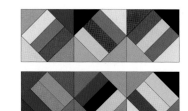

ASSEMBLY
• Fold the patchwork in half, crosswise, right side in. Stitch the 2 ends together, forming a tube.
• Remove the foundation papers.
• Center and press the fusible interfacing circle B to the wrong side of the pouch circle A.
• Keeping the tube inside out, pin it to the bottom circle with the right side of circle A facing the inside of the tube and the interfacing side facing out. Align the raw edges as you stitch all the way around.

For the Lining:

- Fold the lining rectangle in half crosswise, right side in. Leaving a 1 1/2" opening in the center of the side seam, stitch the seam forming a tube.
- Attach the lining circle A to the lining tube, as before.

FINISHING

- With the patchwork bag right side out and lining wrong side out, slip the bag inside the lining, matching the top edge. Stitch all the way around the top.

- Turn the unit right side out through the opening in the lining side seam. Hand stitch the opening closed.
- Tuck the lining inside the patchwork bag. Press the top edge.

To make the casing for the drawstring:

- Fold a 1 3/4" x 4 1/2" bias casing strip in half lengthwise, right side in. Stitch the long side with a 1/4" seam allowance.

Turn it right side out. Fold the ends in and stitch them closed by hand or topstitch by machine. Repeat for the remaining bias casing strip.

- Lay one casing on the right side of the pouch, along the top, about 1/2" from the edge. Topstitch across the lengthwise edges of the bias strip, backstitching securely at each end. Attach the other bias strip in the same manner.

To make the ties:

- Fold a 7/8" x 13" strip in half lengthwise, right side in. Sew the long side to make a tube, using a 1/4" seam allowance. Trim the seam allowance to 1/8" and turn the tube right side out. Make 2. **NOTE:** *Use a loop turner for ease in turning.*
- Thread one tie through both casings and back out on the same side of the bag where it began.

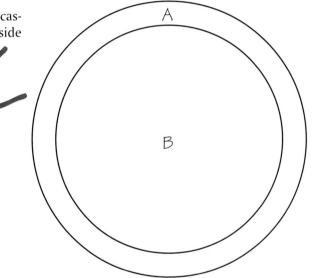

- Beginning at the opening on the other side, thread the remaining tie through both casings and back out the same side where it began. Knot the loose ends of the ties together. Fill your pouch with your favorite collection. To close the bag, pull both ties at once.

Full-Size Patterns for Drawstring Pouch

A

B

Full-Size Foundation Pattern for Drawstring Pouch

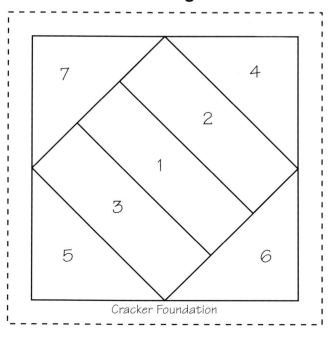

Cracker Foundation

Resource Guide

Ultrasuede (6" x 9" pieces in a variety of colors):
Spiegelhoff's Stretch N' Sew Fabrics
4901 Washington Avenue • Racine, WI 53406
Phone (414)632-2660 • Fax (414)632-0152
http://www.greatcopy.com

New and antique needlework tools:
Anne Powell Ltd.
PO Box 3060 • Stuart, FL 34995 • Phone/Fax (561)287-3007
http://www.annepowellltd.com

Easy Piece (Foundation paper):
Zippy Designs Publishing
RR 1 Box 187M • Newport, VA 24128 • Phone (888)544-7153
Fax (540)544-7071 • http://www.quiltersweb.com

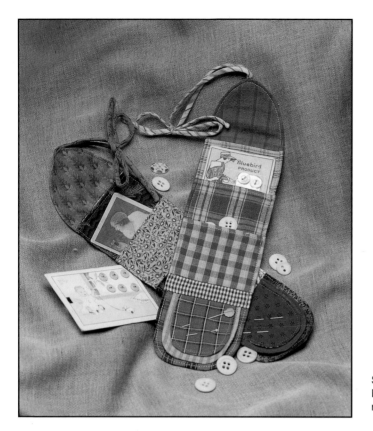

Hanging Needleholder

A place for everything and everything in its place.

Spools of thread, thimbles, needles and pins—all have a pocket to call their own. Hang this needleholder in your sewing room or roll it up and tie it into a convenient bundle.

SIZE: 3" x 11 1/2"

MATERIALS
• Print fabric at least 3 1/2" x 7" for the base foundation
NOTE: *The pockets will be sewn to this piece. It will become the lining of the pockets and the narrow strip that shows just above the needleflaps.*
• Piece of flannel at least 4" x 13" for the backing
• 9 print scraps, each at least 4" square, for the pockets and needle flaps
• Print fabric at least 10" square for the ties (or use ribbon)

CUTTING
Pattern pieces are full size and include a 1/4" seam allowance, as do all dimensions given.
• Cut 1: 3 1/2" x 7" rectangle, print, for the base foundation
• Cut 1: 4" x 13" rectangle, flannel, for the backing
• Cut 2: F, print scraps, for the front flap
• Cut 2: M, print scraps, for the middle flap
• Cut 1: B, print scrap, for the bottom
• Cut 1: T, print scrap, for the top
• Cut 3: 2 1/2" x 3 1/2" rectangles, print scraps, for the pockets
• Cut 2: 1" x 12" bias strips, print, for the ties (or use ribbon)

DIRECTIONS
• Center the 2 F pieces right sides together. Stitch around the curved edge, backstitching at each end. Leave the top open.
• Turn the flap right side out. Press. Topstitch around the curve close to the edge to complete the front flap.
• Repeat for the middle flap using the M pieces.
• Layer the front flap on the middle flap, right sides up. Then place them on the right side of piece B, with the top edges aligned, as shown. Baste across the top, 1/8" from the edge. Set the flap unit aside.
• Narrow hem one long edge of each 2 1/2" x 3 1/2" pocket rectangle in the following manner: press the edge under 1/4". Fold the raw edge under to meet the pressed line and stitch along the fold. Set the pockets aside.
• Fold a 1" x 12" print bias strip in half lengthwise, right side in. Stitch 1/4" from the long raw edge to make a tube. Trim the seam allowance to 1/8" and turn the tube right side out. Make 2. **NOTE:** *Use a loop turner for ease in turning.* Tuck in one end of each tube and hand stitch them closed.

ASSEMBLY
• Measuring from the top of the 3 1/2" x 7" base foundation rectangle, mark 3 lines as indicated in the Pocket Placement Guide.
• Lay the flap unit on the bottom of the base foundation, right sides together, with raw edges aligned. Stitch them together, as shown. Open the unit and press the seam allowance toward the base foundation.
• Lay piece T on the top of the base foundation, right sides together, with raw edges aligned. Stitch them together, leaving a 1 1/2" opening in the center of the seam, as shown.
• Open the unit and press the seam allowance toward the base foundation.
• Follow the lines on the Pocket Placement Guide to place the pockets. Beginning with the upper line, lay a pocket on the

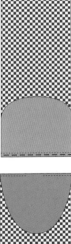

base foundation, right sides together, with the hemmed edge of the pocket toward the bottom and the raw edge along the upper pocket line. Stitch across using a 1/4" seam allowance, as shown. Fold the pocket up along the stitching line and press.

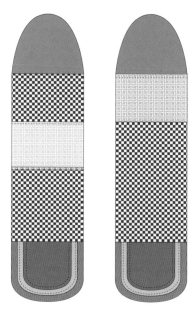

- Repeat for the middle and lower pockets.
- Lay the ties, facing in, with raw edges even, at the top of piece T. Baste the ties

in place and the pockets to the base piece, 1/8" from the edge, as shown.

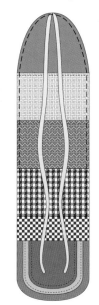

- Lay the needleholder on the 4" x 13" piece of flannel, right sides together. Stitch around the entire outside edge. **NOTE:** *Be careful not to catch the loose ends of the ties or the flaps in your seamline.*
- Trim the excess flannel.
- Turn the needleholder right side out through the opening between the base piece and the top. Press.

- Hand stitch the opening closed.
- Topstitch around the outside, 1/8" from the edge.
- Fill the pockets with thread, thimbles and treasures. Hang your needleholder from a handy knob or roll it up, tie it closed and tuck it in your pocket.

Pocket Placement Guide

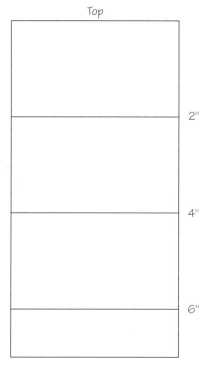

Full-Size Patterns for Hanging Needleholder

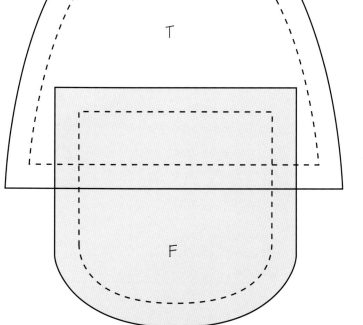

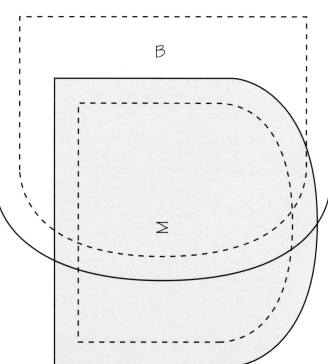

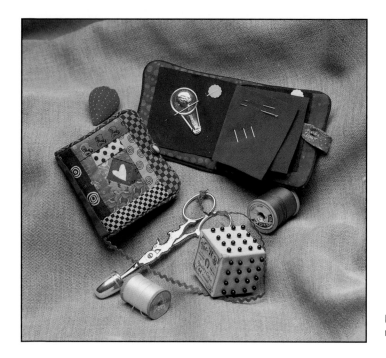

Patchwork Needlebook

A pocket-sized storage system
for your sewing essentials.

Make a folding needlebook with ultrasuede "pages" to secure your pins and needles.

SIZE: 3" square (closed)

MATERIALS
- Light, medium and dark scraps
- 4" x 7" print scrap for the lining
- Scrap of print fabric for the button loop
- 2 pieces of ultrasuede, each 2 1/4" x 4 3/4"
- Paper for foundations
- 4" x 7" piece of thin batting
- 24" baby cording (optional)
- 1/4" button
- 7" strand of pearl cotton

DIRECTIONS
Dimensions include a 1/4" seam allowance. Follow the Foundation Piecing instructions in General Techniques *to make the foundations and to piece the blocks. Make one foundation from pattern A and one from pattern B.*
- If desired, center an initial or small motif in the center of each block. Use assorted print scraps in all remaining positions.

TIP: *Create the texture of quilting without quilting by hand or machine. Place the foundation paper printed side down and layer a piece of thin batting on top of the paper. Piece through the batting and paper—instant quilting!*

ASSEMBLY
- Stitch the two completed blocks together, keeping section 14 of foundation A in the center, as shown. Finger press the seam allowance to one side.

Optional button loop:
- Cut a 2" piece of baby cording. Pull the cord out. Trim the seam allowance to 1/8". Use a loop turner to turn the cording inside out.
- Fold the strip into a small loop. Baste it to the center of one end of the patchwork with the loop facing in.

Full-Size Foundation Patterns for Patchwork Needlebook

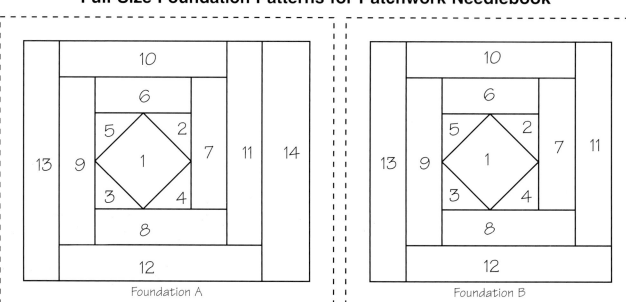

Foundation A

Foundation B

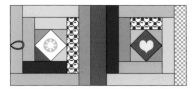

Optional cording:
• Open up the end of the remaining baby cording and trim 1/4" from the end of the cord. Reclose the fabric.

• Lay the patchwork right side up. Align the raw edge of the cording with the edge of the patchwork, beginning in an inconspicuous area, such as the bottom inside edge of the back cover.
• Baste the cording to the patchwork, rounding the corners. Check placement, especially at the corners.
• To hide the seam where the cording will join, tuck the untrimmed end inside the trimmed end, forming one continuous piece of cording.

FINISHING
• Layer the patchwork right side up, lining right side down and the batting (if you haven't already used it) on top of the lining. Turn the stack over.
• Stitch on the basting line, leaving a 1 1/2" opening on one side. Remove the paper foundations.
• Trim the lining and batting even with the edges of the patchwork. Turn the needlebook right side out through the opening. Hand stitch the opening closed.
• Quilt in the ditch.
• Open the needlebook. Layer the two rectangles of ultrasuede and center them inside the needlebook. Use a strand of pearl cotton to sew them to the needle book with a large running stitch.

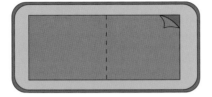

• Sew a button to the back edge corresponding to the button loop.
• Slide a couple of needles and pins into the ultrasuede "pages".

Optional Thimble Pocket:
• Cut 2 pocket pieces, using the pattern given.
• Place them right sides together and stitch, leaving an opening on the top for turning. Turn the pocket right side out and press. Hand stitch the opening closed.
• Hand stitch the pocket to the inside back cover.

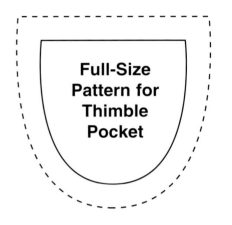

Full-Size Pattern for Thimble Pocket

Notepad

Jot it down, make a list, take a message in style.

Create a cover for a paper notepad. You'll want one by every phone! (I've seen them find their way into purses too.)

SIZE: 3 3/4" x 5" (or custom sized for your paper pad)

MATERIALS
• Assorted print scraps
TIP: *Use appropriate conversation prints to add a personal touch, i.e. musical notes for the piano teacher, ABC fabric for the classroom teacher, etc.*

• Print for the lining at least 8 1/4" x 18"
• Paper for foundations
• 3 1/2" x 5" pad of paper with a cardboard back and front cover
(or any 3 1/4" to 3 1/2"-wide paper pad)

CUTTING
• Cut 6: 1 1/8" x 7" strips, assorted prints
• Cut 1: 4 1/2" x 18" rectangle, print, for

the lining **NOTE:** *Size is approximate. Cut this piece after piecing the notepad cover.*
• Cut 2: 4 1/4" squares, print, for the lining

DIRECTIONS
Follow the Foundation Piecing instructions in General Techniques *to make the foundations and to piece the blocks. Make 2 each of either the Teacup or Cracker foundations on*

pages 24 and 32.

For the Teacup foundation:
• Use the following fabrics in these positions:
    1 - background fabric
    2, 3 - teacup fabric
    4 - background fabric
    5 - teacup fabric
    6 - background fabric
    7 - teacup fabric
    8 - background fabric
    9 - teacup fabric
    10 through 15 - background fabric

For the Cracker foundation:
• Use assorted prints in all positions.

For the Stripe section:
• Stitch the 1 1/8" x 7" print strips together along their length, to make the stripe section, as shown.

NOTE: *Increase or decrease the length of this section to accommodate the thickness of your notepad or a notepad longer or shorter than 5".*

ASSEMBLY
• Stitch a completed foundation to one end of the stripe section. **NOTE:** *If there is a right side up to your foundations keep this in mind as you assemble the pieces.*
• Stitch the remaining foundation to the opposite end of the stripe section, adjusting the length of the stripe section as necessary to accommodate your notepad. The length of the patchwork unit should equal the measurement of the notepad plus 1/2" for ease and 1/2" for the seam allowances.

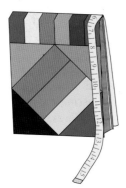

• Stitch a 4 1/4" square of lining fabric to each end of the patchwork unit right

sides together. Press.
• Cut a lining rectangle now, cutting it at least 1/4" larger on all sides than the pieced unit.
• Center the patchwork on the lining, right sides together. Stitch around the outside, leaving a 1 1/2" opening at one end. Trim the lining even with the edges of the patchwork.

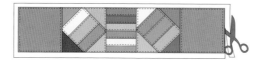

• Remove the paper foundations. Turn the cover right side out. Press. Hand stitch the opening closed.
• Lay the patchwork cover on your work surface lining side up. Center the notepad on it and fold the ends of the

patchwork cover inside the notepad covers. Adjust the patchwork keeping the notepad centered and making sure the ends of the notepad covers extend to the folds when the pad is closed.
• Carefully remove the notepad and pin the end flaps in place. Stitch 1/8" from the edges, securing the end flaps.
• Carefully slip the covers of the notepad into the end flaps.

TIP: *Add a beautiful pen or pencil to complete the gift!*

Full-Size Foundation Patterns for Notepad

(The pattern is continued on page 32.)

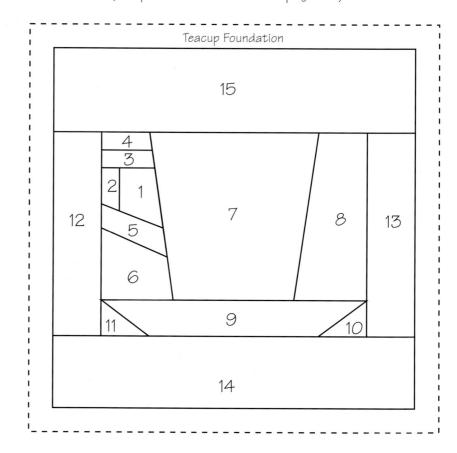

Teacup Foundation

Ball Ornament

Folk art for your Christmas tree!

This intricate-looking ball is easily paper pieced. When quilter friends gathered for a holiday ornament exchange, I was the lucky recipient of this Wendy Hartz original.

SIZE: 4" diameter

MATERIALS
- 5 assorted print scraps, each at least 10 1/2" square (I used gold, purple, green, blue and red)
- 7" square of print fabric for the hanging loop
- Fiberfill
- Paper for the foundations

CUTTING
Dimensions include a 1/4" seam allowance.
- Cut 1: 1" x 9" bias strip, print, for the hanging loop
- Cut 1: 3/4" x 10 1/2" strip, green print, for the center band

TIP: *There are some great conversation prints on the market with messages printed on them, "joy, joy, joy" or "Merry Christmas" for example. This is a perfect place to use them. Adjust the width of the center band to accommodate the words if necessary.*

DIRECTIONS
Follow the foundation piecing instructions in General Techniques to make the foundations and to piece the units. Make 12 foundations of the pattern on page 26.
- Use the following fabrics in these positions:

For each of 6 foundations for the top of the ball ornament:
   1 - gold print
   2, 3 - purple print

For each of 6 foundations for the bottom of the ball ornament:
   1 - red print
   2, 3 - blue print

- After piecing the foundations, stitch 2 top foundations together, starting at point A and ending at point B. Stitch a third top foundation to the pair. Make 2.

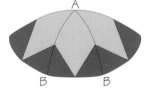

- Fold the 1" x 9" print bias strip in half lengthwise, right side in, and stitch the long side with a 1/4" seam allowance to make a tube. Trim the seam allowance to 1/8" and turn the tube right side out. **NOTE:** *Use a loop turner for ease in turning.*
- Fold the tube in half forming a loop. Baste the ends of the loop to one foundation unit at point A, as shown.

- Lay the foundation units right sides together and stitch, as shown, creating a little "cap."
- Carefully remove the paper foundations.

- Construct the bottom of the ball in the same manner as the top, omitting the hanging loop. Remove the paper foundations.
- Starting 1/2" from one end, stitch the 3/4" x 10 1/2" green print strip to the bottom edge of the top unit, right sides together. Stop stitching 1/2" from where you started. **NOTE:** *If you are using a directional print, take care to place the strip correctly so it will be right side up on the finished ornament.*

- Fold the ends of the strip toward the inside where they meet and pinch to make a crease.

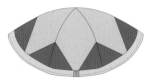

- Place the ends of the strip right sides together, matching creases, and stitch on the crease.
- Trim the excess from the ends of the strip, leaving a 1/4" seam allowance.
- Finish the seam, connecting the strip to the ornament top.

- With right sides together and aligning the gold and red points, sew the bottom half of the ball to the center strip (being careful not to catch the hanging loop in the seam.) Leave a 1" opening.
- Turn right side out through the opening. Stuff firmly with fiberfill. Hand stitch the opening closed.

Full-Size Foundation Pattern for Ball Ornament

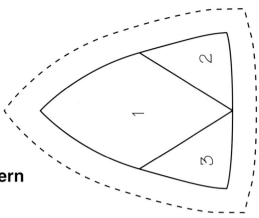

Pin

Tiny scraps can become an heirloom.

Make a tiny piece of your patchwork the center of attention. Paper piecing makes it so simple, you'll even amaze yourself.

SIZE: 1 1/2"

MATERIALS
- Tiny scraps (I used vintage fabrics)
- 1 1/2" wooden heart (available at craft supply stores)
- 2" square of ultrasuede
- Quilting thread
- 1" pin back
- Tacky glue
- Jewelry Glue
- Paper punch
- Paper for the foundation

DIRECTIONS
Follow the Foundation Piecing instructions in General Techniques *to make the foundation and to piece the block. Make one foundation from either of the Heart patterns.*
- Use assorted prints in all positions to piece the heart.

- Center and trace the wooden heart on the paper side of the finished foundation.
- Cut out the heart shape, including a 1/2" allowance.
- Remove the paper foundation.

ASSEMBLY
TIP: *To help prevent the edges of your fabric from ripping, machine stitch just inside the edge of your patchwork before stretching it over the wooden form.*
- Lay the patchwork right side down on your work surface. Center the wooden heart on the foundation.
- Thread a needle with a 24" length of quilting thread. Make a large knot on one end.
- Stretching the patchwork around the wooden form, lace the patchwork diagonally from side to side and from top to

bottom with the quilting thread.

- Pull the thread firmly but not so tight as to tear the fabric.
- Rethread the needle when necessary and lace securely until the back is covered in crisscross lines and the patchwork is stable.
- Trace the heart shape on the ultrasuede, using the finished pin top for a pattern.
- Cut out the heart shape just inside of the traced line.

FINISHING

• Lay the pin back on the ultrasuede and mark a dot under each end of the pin back. Use a paper punch to make a hole in the ultrasuede at each marked dot. (The pin back will be attached to the wooden heart beneath the ultrasuede and the ends will protrude through the holes.)

• Center the ultrasuede heart on the back of the pin top. Make a mark at each hole. Remove the ultrasuede heart.

• Using the jewelry glue, glue the pin back to the back of the wooden heart, aligning the ends of the pin with the marks. Let the glue dry for the recommended time.

• Spread a thin coating of tacky glue over the entire back of the piece. Open the pin, slide the ultrasuede over the pin back and press it onto the back of your pin.

Full-Size Foundation Patterns for Pin

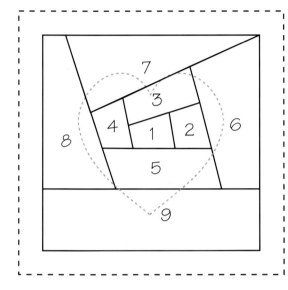

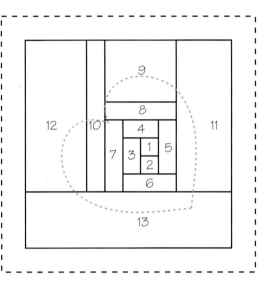

Wooden Patchwork Ornament

Vintage fabrics add charm to simple pieced hearts.

MATERIALS
• Fabric Scraps (I used vintage fabrics)
• Optional: scrap of fabric with a word or hand print your own (See "Printing Fabric" in General Techniques on page 4).
• 8" square of print fabric for the hanging loop
• Wooden heart (available at craft supply stores)
• Quilting thread
• Piece of ultrasuede large enough to cover the back of the wooden form

CUTTING
• Cut 1: 1" x 10" bias strip, print, for the hanging loop

DIRECTIONS
• Trace the wooden heart on a piece of paper. Draw your own foundation pattern, using a free form log cabin design. Start with a center square or rectangle,

considering the size and shape of the printed word if you choose to use one. Continue drawing sections around the center section until the design is 1/2" larger on all sides than the wooden heart.

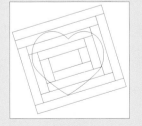

• Piece the heart, using the printed word or other motif in the center position. Use assorted prints in all other positions.
• Fold the 1" x 10" bias strip in half lengthwise, right side in. Stitch the long side to make a tube, using a 1/4" seam allowance. Trim the seam allowance to

1/8" and turn the tube right side out. **NOTE:** *Use a loop turner for ease in turning.*

ASSEMBLY
• Follow the Assembly directions for the pin on page 26.

FINISHING
• Spread a thin layer of glue on the back of the ornament.
• Fold the bias tube in half to make a loop. Lay the loop on the back, with the ends extending approximately 1/2" toward the inside of the heart.
• Add glue to cover the ends of the loop and press the ultrasuede backing in place.

Double Pocket

Tailor these to match your outfit, your mood or the occasion.

Slip your belt through the loop and you have an instant pocket. There are two compartments; one is open at the top and the other is secured with a flap and button.

SIZE: 4 1/2" x 8 1/2"

MATERIALS
- 2 print fabrics, each at least 5" x 14" for the top section
- 2 print fabrics, each at least 5" x 9" for the pocket flap and flap lining
- 2 print fabrics, each at least 5" square for the pocket and lining
- Print scrap at least 2 3/4" square for the button loop
- 3/4" button
- 11" x 17" piece of paper to make the pattern pieces

CUTTING
Pattern pieces are full size and include a 1/4" seam allowance, as do all dimensions given.
- Cut 1: A, from each of 2 prints, for the top section
- Cut 1: B, from each of 2 prints, for the pocket flap and flap lining
- Cut 1: C, from each of 2 prints, for the pocket and lining
- Cut 1: 3/4" x 3" bias strip, print scrap, for the button loop

DIRECTIONS
For Piece #1:
- Place the 2 print A pieces right sides together and stitch from point "a" to point "b", backstitching at each end. Do not sew below the line. Clip the seam allowance to point "a" and point "b."

Clip the seam allowance where indicated and trim the corners.

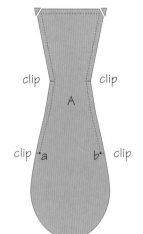

- Turn right side out and press.
- Topstitch 1/8" from the finished edge.

For Piece #2:
- Fold the 3/4" x 3" bias strip in half lengthwise, right side in. Stitch 1/4" from the long raw edge to make a tube. Trim the seam allowance to 1/8" and turn the tube right side out. **NOTE:** *Use a loop turner for ease in turning.*
- Overlap the ends to form a loop.
- Pin the loop to the right side of piece

B at the seam allowance, centering it and keeping the ends toward the outside. **TIP:** *To be sure your button will fit through the loop, try it now and adjust the size of the loop if necessary.*
- Tack the loop to piece B.
- Place the 2 print B pieces right sides

together and stitch from point "c" to point "d", backstitching at each end. Do not sew below the line. Clip the seam allowances at point "c" and point "d". Clip the curve.

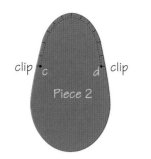

- Turn right side out and press.

For Piece #3:
- Place the 2 print C pieces right sides together and stitch across the top edge. Turn right side out and press.

ASSEMBLY
- Layer the 3 units with the curved raw edges together. Place piece #1 right side up. Next layer piece #3 lining side up. Then layer piece #2 right side up. Stitch all 3 pieces together, around the bottom curve, backstitching at each end. Serge or zigzag the raw edges to finish the seam.

- Turn the pocket right side out, between pieces 1 and 3.
- Fold the top of piece #2 down to make the pocket flap.
- Fold the top of piece #1 down to the top of the pocket flap. Top stitch across (on top of the first top stitching) to secure it, keeping the pocket flap free.

- Sew a button on piece #3 to correspond with the loop.

Full-Size Pattern for Double Pocket
(The patterns are continued on page 30.)

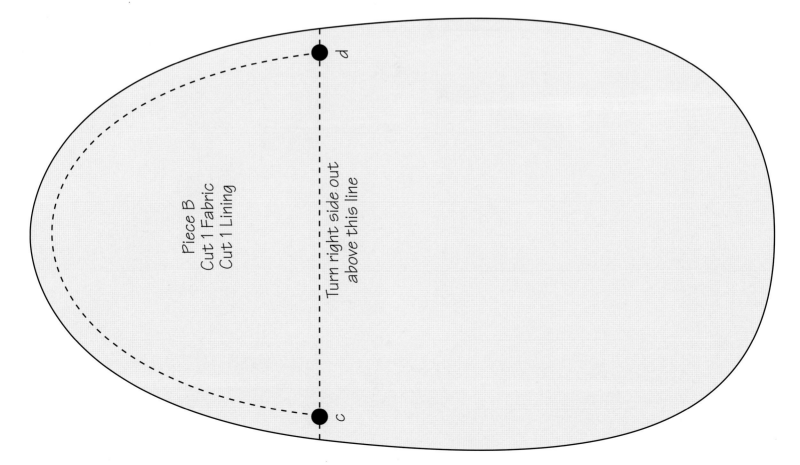

Piece B
Cut 1 Fabric
Cut 1 Lining

Turn right side out above this line

Full-Size Patterns for Double Pocket

(The patterns are continued from page 29.)

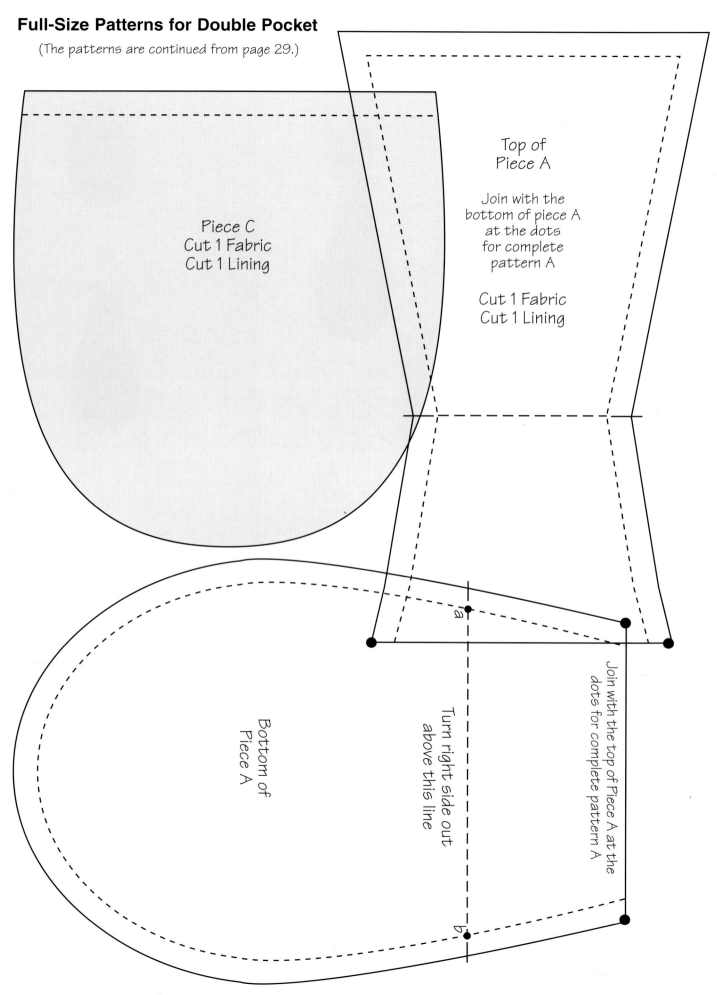

Piece C
Cut 1 Fabric
Cut 1 Lining

Top of
Piece A

Join with the
bottom of piece A
at the dots
for complete
pattern A

Cut 1 Fabric
Cut 1 Lining

a

Bottom of
Piece A

Turn right side out
above this line

b

Join with the top of Piece A at the
dots for complete pattern A

Tea Cozy

A cozy shared warms the heart of a special friend.

Slip this cozy over your teapot to keep your tea hot for hours. No proper tea party should be without one. (I learned that in England!)

SIZE: 9" x 11"

MATERIALS

Yardage is estimated for 44" fabric.
- 48 print scraps totaling approximately 1/2 yard
- 1/2 yard print for the lining
- Print bias strip at least 1 1/2" x 30"
- 15" x 24" piece of batting

TIP: *I used wool batting to enhance the tea cozy's ability to insulate.*
- 11" x 17" piece of paper

PREPARATION

Make a paper pattern from the pattern on page 32. Fold the 11" x 17" piece of paper in half crosswise. Open and place the fold of the paper on the fold line of the pattern. Trace the 1/2 pattern. Refold the paper and cut on the traced line. The pattern includes a 1/4" seam allowance, as do all dimensions given.

NOTE: *This pattern is for a small tea cozy. For a large one, add 3/4" to the curved edge when cutting the pieces out.*

CUTTING

- Cut 48: 2 1/4" x 4" rectangles, assorted prints
- Cut 2: 12" x 15" rectangles, print, for the lining
- Cut 2: 12" x 15" rectangles, wool batting
- Cut 1: 1 1/2" x 30" bias strip, print, for the binding

PIECING

- Stitch eight 2 1/4" x 4" assorted print rectangles into a row, as shown. Press the seam allowances in one direction. Make 6.

ASSEMBLY

- Lay a 12" x 15" lining rectangle right side down. Layer a 12" x 15" rectangle of wool batting on top of the lining.
- Place a row of patchwork on the batting, right side up, as shown.

- Place a row of patchwork on the first row, right sides together. Be sure the seam allowances go in the opposite direction from those in the first row. Turn the top row around if necessary. Stitch through all layers, as shown.

- Open the row and smooth it flat. Place a row of patchwork on the second row, right sides together and checking the direction of the seam allowances. Stitch, as before.

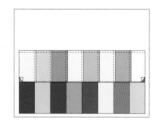

- Open the row and smooth it flat.
- Repeat with the remaining lining and batting rectangles and patchwork rows.
- Lay the paper pattern on top of one patchwork unit, as shown. Cut around the pattern. Repeat for other side. **NOTE:** *If you want your patchwork to match at the seams, be sure to position the pattern in the same place for the front and the back pieces before you cut it out.*

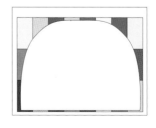

FINISHING

- To make a French seam: Layer the

1/2 Pattern
for Tea Cozy

Fold

patchwork pieces, wrong sides together. Using a scant 1/4" seam, sew around the curved edge of the cozy, backstitching at the bottom edges.

Trim the seam allowance to 1/8".

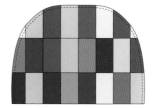

- Turn the cozy inside out.
- Sew around the curved edge of the cozy, using a 1/4" seam allowance and backstitching at both bottom edges. Turn the cozy right side out.
- Lay the bias binding right side down on the Tea Cozy with the raw edges aligned. Starting 1" from the end, stitch the binding to the Tea Cozy with a 1/4" seam allowance. Stop stitching 1" from the starting point.
- Fold the ends of the bias strip toward the wrong side at the point where they meet. Pinch the folds to make creases. Trim the excess from each end, leaving a 1/4" seam allowance.

- Place the ends of the binding strip right sides together and stitch on the crease.
- Finish stitching the binding to the Tea Cozy.
- Turn the binding toward the wrong side of the Tea Cozy. Fold the raw edge of the binding under 1/4" and hand stitch it in place along the stitching line.
- Put the kettle on to boil...

Full-Size Foundation Pattern for Notepad

(The pattern is continued from page 24.)

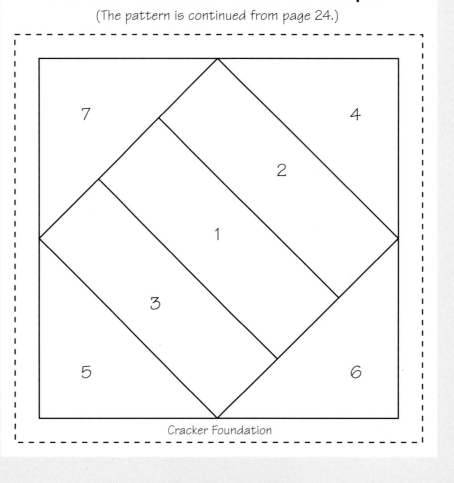

Cracker Foundation